PRINCIPLES
are the *KEYS* to the
KINGDOM
OF GOD

PRINCIPLES
are the *KEYS* to the
KINGDOM OF GOD

EDDIE LEE NAYLOR SR

ReadersMagnet, LLC

Principles Are the Keys to the Kingdom of God
Copyright © 2022 by Eddie Lee Naylor Sr.

Published in the United States of America
ISBN   Paperback: 978-1-959761-17-4
ISBN   eBook: 978-1-959761-18-1

All rights reserved. No part of this publication may be reproduced, stored in a retrieval system or transmitted in any way by any means, electronic, mechanical, photocopy, recording or otherwise without the prior permission of the author except as provided by USA copyright law.

The opinions expressed by the author are not necessarily those of ReadersMagnet, LLC.

ReadersMagnet, LLC
10620 Treena Street, Suite 230 | San Diego, California, 92131 USA
1.619. 354. 2643 | www.readersmagnet.com

Book design copyright © 2022 by ReadersMagnet, LLC. All rights reserved.

Cover design by Ericka Obando
Interior design by Dorothy Lee

TABLE OF CONTENTS

Chapter One - Introduction 7

Chapter Two - Wake-Up Call 14

Chapter Three - Bible Principles 16

Chapter Four - Law Of Polarity 18

Chapter Five - The Principal Of Wisdom 20

Chapter Six - 7 Deadly Sins 23

Chapter Seven - My Story My Story 26

Chapter Eight - Two Certain Paster #1 28

Chapter Nine - Old Testament 32

Chapter Ten - Old and New Testament 36

Chapter Eleven - What Is Tithing? 40

Chapter Twelve - The Principles Of Tithing 42

Chapter Thirteen - Tithing Is A Perfected Principal 46

Chapter Fourteen - Principle Number 2 48

Chapter Fifteen - Tithing Is A Blesssd Principle 49

Chapter Sixteen - The Ten Principles Of Tithing 51

Chapter Seventeen - Tithing Church and Job 53

Chapter Eighteen - Providing For Those In Need 55

Chapter Nineteen - Principle Five Local Churches 56

Chapter Twenty - Tithe Is Built Into The Framework Of Humanity ... 57

Chapter Twenty One - Tithing Is An Eternal Princple 61

Chapter Twenty-Two - God Does Not Ask Less of Us 62

Chapter Twenty-Three - Should Not Be Approached Legalistically 63

Chapter Twenty-Four - Tithing Should Be a Minimum 63

Chapter Twenty-Five - Tithing Opens Up Blessings.. 64

Chapter Twenty-Six - Tithing is About Obedience 65

Chapter Twenty-Seven - Jesus Spoke In Parables 70

Chapter Twenty-Eight - The Father Spoke In Parables... 71

Chapter Twenty-Nine - What Was A Blood Covenant? 72

Chapter Thirty - Our Covenant In Christ... 75

Chapter Thirty-One - The Covenant Is Mediated To All Of Mankind............... 78

INTRODUCTION

As simple as it sounds, one of the greatest proofs of God's existence is the ability to choose. Materialistic God-deniers hypothesize that all of our actions can be attributed to random interactions of the chemicals, atoms, and molecules that make up our physical bodies. However, they are unable to explain how such random interactions lead to our ability to make all kinds of decisions in life.

Little wonder why when God created man in His image, He put Adam and Eve in a position where they, like God who chose to become flesh in the form of Jesus Christ had the ability to choose for themselves are all familiar with the story of how they made a poor choice in eating the forbidden fruit for which God held them both accountable. Think about it! Would God have held Adam and Eve accountable for their poor choice if their actions were the result of random chemical interactions!

Personally, I believe that a desire to avoid accountability is a major reason many people are drawn to a materialistic-atheistic world view. Furthermore, they don't understand that God created and designed us to make choices.

In the Bible, there are more than 200 references to the word "choose" or one of its variations. This makes it possible for God to fulfill His role as the Supreme Judge of the universe as illustrated in Deuteronomy 30:19 and yet give us freedom to make decisions: *"I call heaven and earth as witnesses against you today that I have set before your life and death, blessing and curse. Choose life so that you and your descendants may live…"*

Later, in a New Testament passage, the author of Hebrews warns: *"Make sure that you do not reject the One who speaks. For if they did not escape when they rejected Him who warned them on earth, even less will we if we turn away from Him who warns us from heaven"* (Hebrews 12:25).

We must also remember that because we have the ability and freedom to choose, our actions have consequences. I establish a bridge between the Old and New Testament applications of this truth:

The author then reminded them of God's holy presence at Mount Sinai when the old covenant was revealed. It was a terrifying experience (Exodus 19:9-16; 20:18). How much more dreadful the situation for all unbelievers who someday will be judged severely for rejecting the Messiah... However, the good news is that we can spend eternity with God, not because of our good works but because we have received God's free gift of salvation.

Truly, the choices we make-especially those that are spiritual and moral in nature — serve as reminders that we are made in God's image.

"The keys of the Kingdom," sometimes called "the keys to the kingdom," represent the authority to open the way for people to "enter into the Kingdom of God." (Matthew 16:19; Acts 14:22) Jesus gave Peter "the keys of the Kingdom of the heavens." This means that Peter received the authority to unlock information about how faithful people, by receiving God's Holy Spirit, could enjoy the privilege of entering the Kingdom in heaven.

FOR WHOM WERE THE KEYS USED?

Peter used authority from God to open the way for three groups to enter the Kingdom:

Jews and Jewish converts. Shortly after Jesus' death, Peter encouraged a crowd of Jewish believers to accept Jesus as the one selected by God to rule in the Kingdom. Peter showed them what they must do to get saved. He thus opened the way for them to enter the Kingdom, and thousands "accepted his word." -Acts 2:38-41.

Samaritans. Peter was later sent to the Samaritans. He again used a key of the Kingdom when he, along with the apostle John, "prayed for them to get Holy Spirit." (Acts 8:14-17) This opened the way for the Samaritans to enter the Kingdom.

Gentiles. Three and a half years after Jesus' death, God revealed to Peter that Gentiles (non-Jews) would also have the opportunity to enter the Kingdom. In response, Peter used one of the keys by preaching to Gentiles, thus opening the door for them to receive the holy spirit, become Christians, and be prospective members of the Kingdom. -Acts 10:30-35,44, 45.

What does it mean to "enter into the Kingdom"?

Those who actually "enter into the Kingdom" become co rulers with Jesus in heaven. The Bible foretold that they would "sit on thrones" and "rule as kings over the earth." -Luke 22:29, 30; Revelation 5:9, 10.

MISCONCEPTIONS ABOUT THE KEYS OF THE KINGDOM

Misconception: Peter decides who may enter heaven.

Fact: The Bible says that Christ Jesus, not Peter, "is to judge the living and the dead." (2 Timothy 4:1, 8; John 5:22) In fact, Peter himself said that Jesus "is the one decreed by God to be judge of the living and the dead." - Acts 10:34, 42.

Misconception: Heaven waited on Peter to decide when to use the keys of the Kingdom.

Fact: When Jesus spoke about the keys of the Kingdom, he told Peter: "Whatever you bind on earth shall be bound in heaven; and whatever you loose on earth shall be loosed in heaven." (Matthew 16:19) Although some understand this statement to mean that Peter dictated decisions to heaven, the original Greek verbs show that Peter's decisions would *follow* those made in heaven rather than precede them.

The Bible elsewhere shows that Peter was subject to heaven when using the keys of the Kingdom. For example, he responded to instructions from God when using the third key.—Acts 10:19, 20.

At times, the Bible uses the term "key" as a symbol of authority and responsibility.—Isaiah 22:20-22; Revelation 3:7, 8.

The Samaritans belonged to a religion that was distinct from Judaism but that incorporated some teachings and practices from the Mosaic Law.

KEYS TO THE KINGDOM

"And I will give unto thee the keys of the Kingdom of Heaven: and whatsoever thou shalt bind on earth shall be bound in Heaven: and whatsoever thou shalt loose on earth shall be loosed in Heaven." (Matthew 16:19)

PRINCIPLES

<u>The secret to accessing the things of the Kingdom is to have the right keys. Not literal keys of course, but principles that open the floodgates of Heaven.</u> "

AN APPOINTED KINGDOM

before Jesus returned to Heaven He told His disciples:

"And I appoint unto you a Kingdom, as my Father hath appointed unto me." (Luke 22:29).

Jesus also spoke of His Church which would extend the message of the Kingdom throughout the world:

"And I say also unto thee, that thou art Peter, and upon this rock I will build my church; and the gates of Hell shall not prevail against it. And I will give unto thee the keys of the Kingdom of Heaven: and whatsoever thou shalt bind on earth shall be bound in Heaven; and whatsoever thou shalt loose on earth shall be loosed in Heaven." (Matthew 16:18-19)

In passage above Jesus revealed that Peter would be one of the spiritual foundation stones of the first church. This meant he would be a vital part of its growth and development. Peter's name actually meant "a rock" or "stone." Jesus then said of Himself, "...upon this rock I will build my Church" indicating that the Church would derive its existence from Him. He would be the rock upon which the Church was built.

There would be many other lesser stones (people like Peter). These stones would be an important part of the Church. But Jesus Himself was the cornerstone on which the structure of the Church was to be built. Jesus then made two comments regarding this Church.

First, He said that "the gates of Hell shall not prevail against it." This implied that the Church would have enemies fighting it, but assured that the enemies would not overcome it.

Second, and most important to our study, Jesus promised to give the keys to His Kingdom to the Church.

In the natural world if you possess the keys to a building, it means you have authority there. <u>The authority Jesus was speaking of in this passage is a spiritual authority. He gave the Church spiritual keys to the doors of His Kingdom. Jesus said "I" will give them.</u>

The power and authority of the Church was to flow from Jesus. The use of the word "will" (future tense) meant that the keys had not yet been given at the time Jesus spoke. This power was released in Acts 2 when the Holy Ghost was given to believers:

" But ye shall receive power, after that the Holy Ghost is come upon you: and ye shall be witnesses unto me both in Jerusalem, and in all Judaea, and in Samaria, and unto the uttermost part of the earth." (Acts 1:8)

<u>The keys to the Kingdom were the power to bind and loose. To bind something means to put fetters or a bond on it. It is like closing and locking the door to a room. To loose something is to release or set it free. It is similar to opening the door to a room.</u>

The secret keys to kingdom things are position and disposition. Disposition is Kingdom Citizenship. Position is righteousness. Position and disposition: those are the keys. Get your citizenship in order and then stay in right relationship with the heavenly country and all these things will be added to you".

The Church would have a position of authority. It would have the keys to God's Kingdom. It would be the instrument through which the spiritual doors to the Kingdom would be opened to the nations of the world.

HOW TO ENTER THE KINGDOM?

The keys to the Kingdom were given by Jesus to the Church. But specifically, how was entrance to be gained to the Kingdom of God?

John 3:1-21 records the story of Nicodemus, a religious leader at the time of Christ's ministry on earth. He came to Jesus desiring to gain access to the Kingdom of God and, by doing so, inherit eternal life. Jesus told him:

"Verily, verily, I say unto thee, except a man is born again, he cannot see the Kingdom of God." (John 3:3)

Nicodemus was confused. He asked Jesus:

"How can a man are born when he is old? Can he enter the second time into his mother's womb, and be born?" (John 3:4)

Jesus explained to Nicodemus that the "born-again" experience of which He spoke was not a physical birth. Through physical birth you are born into a kingdom of this world as a citizen of a nation.

At natural birth, you inherit the basic sin nature:

"Behold, I was shaped in iniquity; and in sin did my mother conceive me." (Psalms 51:5)

Because God's Kingdom is a spiritual kingdom, you must be born into it through spiritual rebirth. You must change your residency from the kingdom of Satan to the Kingdom of God. Jesus said:

"That which is born of the flesh is flesh: and that which is born of the Spirit is Spirit. Marvel not that I said unto thee, ye must be born again." (John 3:6-7)

Paul explained that you could not enter the Kingdom with a flesh and blood body:

"Now this I say, brethren, that flesh and blood cannot inherit the Kingdom of God..." (I Corinthians 15:50)

You enter the Kingdom of God and become heirs of the Kingdom through spiritual rebirth. The way to be born again is by believing that Jesus died to pay the penalty for your sins. You must confess your sins, ask forgiveness, be baptized into his church and place your trust in Him:

"For God so loved the world, that He gave His only begotten Son, that whosoever believeth in Him should not perish, but have everlasting life.

For God sent not His Son into the world to condemn the world; but that the world through Him might be saved. "(John 3:16-17)

It is through Jesus that you can move from the kingdom of Satan to the Kingdom of God:

"(God) Who hath delivered us from the power of darkness and hath translated us into the Kingdom of His Dear Son." (Colossians 1:13)

REPENTANCE OR REVOLUTION?

When Jesus came to earth to extend the Kingdom of God, some who acknowledged Him as King thought the Kingdom would come through revolution. They thought there would be an actual physical revolt against the existing ruling powers of the world. But Jesus taught that the key to His Kingdom was not revolution but repentance (Changing the way you used to think and think the kingdom way):

"Jesus answered, My Kingdom is not of this world: if my Kingdom were of his world, then would my servants fight that I should not be delivered to the Jews: but now is my Kingdom not from hence."(John 18:36)

"Now after that John was put in prison, Jesus came into Galilee, preaching the Gospel of the Kingdom of God.

And saying the time is fulfilled, and the Kingdom of God is at hand: repent you, and believe the Gospel. (Mark 1:14-15)

From that time Jesus began to preach, and to say, Repent: for the Kingdom of Heaven is at hand."

CHAPTER TWO

WAKE-UP CALL

Again in the human world Jesus second coming is upon humankind again it is "WAKE-UP TIME FOR THE LAST TIME" before He comes again for mankind "DON'T BE LETT BEHIND".

"Now after that John was put in prison, Jesus came into Galilee, preaching the Gospel of the Kingdom of God.

And saying the time is fulfilled, and the Kingdom of God is at hand: repent you, and believe the Gospel. (Mark 1:14-15)

From that time Jesus began to preach, and to say, Repent: for the Kingdom of Heaven is at hand."

This trumpet is being blown again in our time.

PRINCIPALES ARE BEING TAUGHT AGAIN AND WHAT HAPPEN IF YOU USE THE WROUNG KEY. AND WHERE USING THE WRONG KEY WILL TAKE YOU!!!

"The keys of the Kingdom," sometimes called "the keys to the kingdom," represent the authority to open the way for people to "enter into the Kingdom of God."

God is trying to give us the keys to the kingdom of Heaven through Jesus Christ.

God is trying to give us the keys to open the widows of Heaven though Jesus Christ so that He can pour us out a blessing that we will not have room to contain.

God is trying to take us to the promise land.

God is trying to kill all the giants in your land.

God is killing the giant of Tithing.

I am going do you want to go?

To unlock your car or house it only takes one key for you to gain access.

Fact: When Jesus spoke about the keys of the Kingdom, he told Peter: "Whatever you bind on earth shall be bound in heaven; and whatever you loose on earth shall be loosed in heaven." Matthew 16:19).

PRINCIPLES

the secret to accessing the things of the Kingdom is to have the right keys. Not literal keys of course, but principles that open the floodgates of Heaven. "

CHAPTER THREE

BIBLE PRINCIPLES

BIBLE PRINCIPLE

A biblical principle is a principle founded in the bible. For example, faith; which is a lifestyle is also a biblical principle. It comprises of believing and confessing you have received what you believe for before you physically receive it.

Bible principles are fundamental truths

THE TEN COMMANDMENTS ARE BIBLE PRINCIPLES.

"God requires personal, perfect, perpetual obedience to His revealed will. [And] Where do we find God's revealed will regarding moral conduct? The biblical answer is that it is summarized in the Ten Commandments" (pg. 70). For the Christian, Jesus has obeyed the Law for us and has taken the curse of the Law for us, living, dying, and rising again to save us. <u>We are justified by faith in His person and work; but, before we are even able to trust in Him by faith</u>

we need to be born again, we need a new heart. And God gives us one so that we will trust in Him and then live for Him.

3. Which two principles are primary?

Jesus spoke of two principles of prime importance. The first reveals the very purpose of human life—to know God, to love him, and to serve him faithfully. This first principle should be considered in all our decisions. (Proverbs 3:6) Those who take this principle to heart gain friendship with God, true happiness, and everlasting life. —Read Matthew 22:36-38.

The second principle can guide us into peaceful relationships with others. (1 Corinthians 13:4-7) Applying this second principle involves imitating God's way of treating people.—Read Matthew 7:12; 22:39, 40.

4. How do Bible principles benefit us?

Principle definition: 1. a basic idea or rule that explains or controls how something happens or works: 2. if you agree with or believe something in principle, you agree with the idea in general, although you might not support it in reality or in every situation: 3. a moral rule or standard of good....

Principle is normally used as a noun meaning 'a fundamental basis of a system of thought or belief', as in this is one of the basic principles of democracy.

A principle is a concept or value that is a guide for behavior or evaluation. In law, it is a rule that has to be or usually is to be followed, or can be desirably followed, or is an inevitable consequence of something, such as the laws observed in nature or the way that a system is constructed. The principles of such a system are understood by its users as the essential characteristics of the system, or reflecting system's designed purpose, and the effective operation.

LAWS

Laws, on the other hand, may be for specific circumstances. (Deuteronomy 22:8) We must use thinking ability to understand how a principle applies in a particular situation. (Proverbs 2:10-12) For example, the Bible teaches that life is a gift from God. That basic principle can guide us at work, at home, and while traveling. It leads us to take safety precautions.—Read Acts 17:28.

CHAPTER FOUR

LAW OF POLARITY

An understanding of the Principle will enable one to change his own Polarity (DIRECTION), as well as that of others, if he will devote the time and study necessary to master the art.

LAW OF POLARITY

The law Polarity is a universal law it has two directions that is diametrical opposed to each other like God and the Devil, Heaven or Hell, Good or Bad, Right or Wrong.

"Everything in the universe has its opposite. You have a right and left side to your body, front and back.

Every up has a down and every down has an up. It is equal and opposite. If it was 3 feet from the floor up on to the table, it would 3 feet from the table down to the floor. If it is 150 miles from North Carolina to South Carolina, then it must be 150 miles to North Carolina; it could be any other way.

If something you considered bad happens in your life, there has to be something good about it. If it was only a little bad, when you mentally work your way around to the other side, you will find it will only be a little good.

Let your life represent any situation that you are living now. Remember that every situation JUST IS, you make it negative or positive by virtue of how you choose to think with principals about the situation.

When you look at the situation one way and it is negative, you can change your perspective and look at it from the opposite viewpoint or side and find that it will be positive.

Remember polarity is about choosing "DIRECTIONS" in life. The word of God tells us to choose life.

Deuteronomy 30:19 - I call heaven and earth to record this day against you, that I have set before you life and death, blessing and cursing: therefore choose life, that both thou and thy seed may live:

John 10:10 - The thief cometh not, but for to steal, and to kill, and to destroy: I am come that they might have life, and that they might have it more abundantly.

Jeremiah 1:5 - Before I formed thee in the belly I knew thee; and before thou camest forth out of the womb I sanctified thee, and I ordained thee a prophet unto the nations.

Romans 6:23 - For the wages of sin is death; but the gift of God is eternal life through Jesus Christ our Lord.

2 Peter 3:9 - The Lord is not slack concerning his promise, as some men count slackness; but is longsuffering to us-ward, not willing that any should perish, but that all should come to repentance.

John 3:16 - For God so loved the world, that he gave his only begotten Son, that whosoever believeth in him should not perish, but have everlasting life.

Acts 17:30 - And the times of this ignorance God winked at; but now commandeth all men every where to repent:

Exodus 4:11 - And the LORD said unto him, Who hath made man's mouth? or who maketh the dumb, or deaf, or the seeing, or the blind? have not I the LORD?

CHAPTER FIVE

THE PRINCIPAL OF WISDOM

9 REASONS WHY WISDOM IS THE PRINCIPAL THING

The quest for knowledge is among the most sought after thing in the world today whether through the reading of books, magazines, television, social media, research and experiments, just to mention a few.

How many though would exert that same level of enthusiasm or energy in their effort to get wisdom? It is good to have knowledge yes, because that is the will of God for our lives yet it is more profitable when we explore every opportunity afforded us to get wisdom.

There was one who had such an opportunity. His name was Solomon. He was the son of David and was an extremely rich man. [2 Chronicles 1:14-17] He established himself securely over all his kingdom and the bible said the Lord his God was with him and made him exceeding great.

He ruled over Israel and the favor of God was much upon him. In 2 Chronicles 1: 7 we read how on the night when God appeared to him, Solomon was given the chance to ask God for even more blessings and favor upon his life.

SOLOMON'S CHOICE WORDS

He was told by the Lord God, *"Ask what I shall give to you." 2 Chronicles 1:7*

Now you're probably thinking if that was you, you would ask God for trillions of dollars – some what like the jackpot, right? That way you can buy whatever you want in this life.

Quite naturally, one would think that here is a man who is already 'filthy' rich and given this once in a lifetime chance, he would ask God for more riches, possessions, honor, personal glory, long life or perhaps even ask for the life of all his haters.

But instead Solomon said to God, "You have shown me great loving-kindness and mercy to my father David, and have made me king in his place. Now, O Lord God, your promise to my father David is fulfilled, for You have made me king over a people as numerous as the dust of the earth. Give me wisdom and knowledge, so that I may go out and come in [performing my duties] before this people, for [otherwise] who can rule and administer justice to this great people of yours?" 2 Chronicles 1:8-10 AMP

The bible says that God was so pleased with Solomon's prayer request that not only did He grant him the desire of his heart for wisdom and knowledge, God gave him far more riches and possessions that surpassed all of the wealth and riches of others.

"Wisdom and knowledge have been granted you. I will also give you riches, possessions, and honor, such as none of the kings who were before you has possessed nor will those who will come after you." [2 Chronicles 1:12]

WHY WISDOM IS THE PRINCIPAL THING

In the book of Proverbs 4:7 ASV it says, "Wisdom is the principal thing; therefore, get wisdom; Yea, with all thy getting get understanding."

It is interesting to note that the author of the book of Proverbs is the man Solomon himself! The invitation that he gives is for his children to come and receive instructions from him. (Proverbs 4:1-2).

Solomon desired that his children would grow up to have wisdom and knowledge in the same proportion as he himself had been gifted by God. Wisdom is preeminent and we must desire to attain it in a very skilful and godly manner.

God gives it liberally when we ask of Him. The writer of James says, "If any man lacks wisdom, [to guide him through a decision or circumstance] let him ask of God, that grivet to all men liberally [freely] and upbraided not [without rebuke or blame]; and it shall be given him." ~ James 1:5 KJV

Along with wisdom it is our duty to also get understanding – to actively seek spiritual discernment, mature comprehension and logical interpretation that can come to us only through the word of God. Here are 10 things that we all need wisdom for –

Wisdom to know and to love God first/foremost and have a relationship with Him (Genesis 1:26-27; Deuteronomy 6:5)

Wisdom to discern truth (John 8:32)

Wisdom to do God's will (Romans 12:2)

Wisdom is the key that unlocks the vault of God's treasures (Colossians 2:3)

Wisdom to love your wives

Wisdom to know what to say and when to say it (James 1:5)

Wisdom to raise your children and keep them on the right path (Proverbs 22:6)

Wisdom to administer justice (2 Chronicles 1:10)

Wisdom to solve problems (Proverbs 3:5)

Wisdom to make the right choices and decisions (Proverbs 11:14)

CHAPTER SIX

7 DEADLY SINS

SEVEN THINGS THAT GOD HATE

(Key-verses: Proverbs 6:16-19)

When reading God"s Word our tendency is to turn first to the passages which bring comfort and encouragement. Sometimes, however, it is necessary to turn to those verses ""useful for teaching, rebuking, correcting and training…" …" -- look up 2 Timothy 3:16-17. These verses bring before us the kind of teaching we are always needing, so before examining the seven things which God hates, let's make three observations about this portion of scripture.

1. *These verses clearly emphasise the moral hideousness of the human heart and of the world in which we live.* The seven evils mentioned are all around us. These verses, therefore, declare the depravity of man. This is not a popular subject and in many quarters is no longer believed; but whether men believe that the human race is depraved or not, it does not alter the fact. It is all too apparent as we watch trends in literature, programmes on television, and the kinds of pictures and plays which are advertised. Wherever we look we see

the great sinfulness of sin (Isaiah 1:5-6; Jeremiah 17:9). How great is the moral hideousness of the human heart!

2. *These verses remind us of the holiness and purity of God and of His hatred of sin.* These are the seven sins which are called ""detestable"". How much does God hate sin? In a former dispensation God hated sin so much that He destroyed most of the human race which He had created (Genesis 6:5-7). But to find out how much God hates sin we must look at Calvary to remind ourselves that so great was the divine hatred against sin that God actually surrendered His Own Son to the fearful suffering and anguish of a Roman gibbet, so that sin might once and for all be dealt with — look up Philippians 2:8. How holy God is, and how much He hates sin!

3. *These verses remind us that the true ambition and desire of God"s people is, or should be, to live without these offensive sins which God hates.* Thank God, it is possible to live a life that is pleasing to Him! He has provided victory over all the things that grieve Him. We are to be different people, and we may be (Romans 8:37; Ephesians 4:30).

What, then, are the seven things that God hates?

1. A Proud Look — ""haughty eyes""

Pride is the primary sin (James 4:6). It was through pride that the Devil fell. What an insidious thing pride is! That is why the Apostle Peter speaks about the virtue of humility (1 Peter 3:4; 5:5). What did Jesus say in Matthew 11:29-30?

2. A Lying Tongue

But surely Christians do not lie? Unfortunately, they do sometimes. But surely it's alright to tell "white" lies? Is it? God hates "" a lying tongue"". But surely it's impossible to get on in business these days without telling the occasional lie? God hates ""a lying tongue""; see what Paul wrote in Ephesians 4:25. We need to pray David's prayer in Psalm 120:2.

3. Heartless Cruelty — ""hands that shed innocent blood""

We quite naturally think of Cain and Abel (Genesis 4:1-15). In the New Testament we read about Cain, who shed innocent blood when he killed Abel (1 John 3:11-12,15). Do you hate anyone? Then in God"s sight you are a murderer, and God hates murderers.

4. Vicious Scheming — ""a heart that devises wicked schemes""

We are reminded here of the source of evil which begins inside. See what Jesus said (Matthew 15:18-19). How different was Dorcas in Acts 9:36; and Barnabas (Acts 11:24).

5. Mischievous Eagerness — ""feet that are quick to rush into evil""

Here are feet that run to do mischief! This is the Devil's work because he ""prowls around like a roaring lion"" (1 Peter 5:8). God hates this mischief. What are your feet doing? Are they the beautiful feet of Romans 10:15?

6. Social Slander — ""a false witness who pours out lies""

An old writer has said, "This is an accursed thing! It works oftentimes by other means than words: by a look or a shrug of the shoulders it levels its poisoned arrows; it has broken many a virtuous heart and stained many a virtuous reputation. It has nodded away many a good name, and winked into existence a host of suspicions, that have gathered round and crushed the most chaste and virtuous of our kind. It often works in the dark, and generally under the mask of truthfulness and love."" God hates slander -- see what He says about it in Ephesians 4:29 and 32.

7. Divisive Strife — "a man who stirs up dissension among brothers""

This perhaps is the worst of the seven sins. Another old writer refers to the man who "by "tale bearing, untrue stories, half-truths, subtle insinuations, produces the disruption of friendships and the break-up of fellowship…" …" God hates this!

This is a dreadful subject but perhaps it is needed, and we must ask the question, how can we be released from these things which God hates and filled with those things which He loves?

1. We must be honest with ourselves and with God; let the searchlight of His Word and of the Holy Spirit come into our hearts and reveal the things which displease Him. Then we must admit our wrong, confess our sin and forsake that which grieves the Lord (2 Corinthians 7:1).

2. We must seek and receive the cleansing of Christ's precious blood. Thank God, this is available for the saint and for the sinner! (1 John 1:7).

3. We must rely upon the Holy Spirit for victory (2 Corinthians 3:17).

CHAPTER SEVEN

MY STORY MY STORY

MY STORY

As long as I have been a Christian since 1974 when I was born-again, I can remember people arguing and debating about tithing.

Some say it was only an Old Testament Law that doesn't need to be followed as believers under the New Covenant.

And some say that tithing is just as relevant to New Testament Christians as it was in the Old Covenant.

My goal with this page is to shine a light on what the Bible says about tithing (in both the New and Old testament) and answer many questions you may have about it.

I tapped into the wisdom of others who have studied this subject out to great depths and hopefully we can better see what we as New Testament Christians need to know about tithing.

HOW CAN YOU BELIEVED IN TITHING WITHOUT UNDERSTANDING THE PRINCIPLE?

I argued and disputing about tithing for years' preachers that preached tithing was personional entertainers that only wanted to line their own pockets. They were taking money from people that was in debt, needing food and in poverty. I was one of these people needing God to bless me. I wanted to believe in the Word of God. I needed to believe that Malachi 3:10 was true dapperly. I needed to know I could stand in faith on God word. But I kept getting worse, my situation was not improving. I did not know what I was doing wrong, until I got in the word of God.

CHAPTER EIGHT

TWO CERTAIN PASTER #1

PASTOR CREFLO DOLLAR

Then I heard a revelating about tithing that shook my tithing faith again. In the middle of a famine, gas shortage, inflation, war, climate, earth quakes, gun shootings, murder, high interest rates, rapes, diseases and much much more. In the 21 century on July 5, 2022 a certain American Preacher is reportedly catching heat from other pastors about this very same subject after admitting to his congregants that he lied to them about tithing.

In a new video, the pastor served up a sermon on Sunday at the 30,000-member Church International that was titled, "The Great Misunderstanding."

"Today I stand in humility to correct some things I've taught for years and believed for years," he says in the video.

<u>He went on to explain that tithing is no longer relevant for New Testament believers as it is a law of the Old Testament.</u>

He cited Romans 6: 14 to stress that Christians live under grace and not the laws of the Old Testament. This very same pastor calls on congregation to send tithes via Cash APP Amid Coronavirus Chaos.

Romans 6: 14: "For sin shall not have dominion over you; for ye are not under the law, but under the grace."

Tithing is when you give 10% of your income to your local church. "He said the manufactured 10% figure is all wrong," "He says I want you to take a portion and put it aside. Now if you want to give 10% that's fine but, you know, he didn't say that," He said in the June 26 video.

"You are under grace not under laws," he said.

In a sermon titled 'The Great Misunderstanding' from June 26th this year, this pastor has publicly admitted that he misled congregants on tithing teachings.

During the Sunday service, the pastor said: "I will say that I have no shame at all at saying to you throw away every book, every tape, and every video I ever did on the subject of tithing. Unless it lines up with this [the Bible].

"I've done some corrective teaching in the last ten years, but not to the degree of what we're getting ready to do now.

"So why is this important? Because religion is sustained by two factors, fear and guilt. And if there's one subject that the Church has used, for a long time, to keep people in fear and guilt, it is in that subject of tithing, and it has to be corrected. And it's got to be corrected now."

The pastor said he might lose some professional engagements after his confession but added that this was something that he's been through.

Misunderstanding," the prosperous pastor, who has received millions in donations over the years, told his devout followers to toss out all their books, tapes, and videos of him teaching the practice.

According to his teaching on tithing is not biblical and he argued that churchgoers should not feel obligated to set aside a portion of their income in order to give back.

Meanwhile, Pastor slammed his flip flop on tithing.

"Until he has a "Zacchaeus" spirit which involves giving the people a REFUND for all the tapes, videos, books, and other materials they bought from him, I am not moved by his "new" revelation on tithing that is still flawed. It's flawed because #Jesus Christ used the "law" in His teachings.

For example: In Matthew 4:4,7, & 10, whenever Jesus said, "It is written…" that was the law being used to combat the temptations of the devil. Study to ShowThyselfApproved," the pastor said, as reported by by the news.

As noted by the news he has a jet that "comes with two Rolls-Royce engines, high-speed Internet and two multichannel satellites and allows for a four-and-a-half-hour commute from New York to Los Angeles."

The pastor is changing direction, doing a 180 in his trajectory of thought, years after he took fire for asking his parishioners to donate $300 each so he could buy a $65 million Gulfstream G650 jet for doing ministry abroad.

In his ministry, he uses a term called "Honor Giving" which is akin to tithing that was reported.

Many have accused him of enriching himself "on the backs of credulous, lower-income worshippers." Many took to face book to call him out. They said, "Until he has a "Zacchaeus" spirit which involves giving the people a REFUND for all the tapes, videos, books, and other materials they bought from him, I am not moved by his "new" revelation on tithing that is still flawed.

Check out the video and let us know your thoughts.

He is the senior pastor and founder of a large church.

He is estimated to have a net worth of $27 million, most of which came from his ministerial establishments around the United States.

He has International covenant association, Arrow records, and the other ministries are jointly overseen by the popular TV evangelist and his wife.

In 1984, he was awarded a Bachelor degree in sciences by a West Georgia College. Oral Roberts University awarded him an honorary doctorate degree in 1998. His ministry's first ever gathering was held in a cafeteria with only eight people in attendance.

In that meeting, the pastor was said to have raised $100 from the participants. In 2006, the overall cash revenue received in his church was about $69 million. His congregation has grown in leaps and bounds over the years, today his ministry boasts of over 30, 000 members. His church auditorium was built with $18 million without any bank loans. He is the publisher of a Magazine with over 100,000 readers around the US.

The Pastor apologized for all the years he taught tithing incorrectly and said religion is sustained by two things: fear and guilt.

The famous Pastor has not yet offered restitution — redistribution of his amassed wealth from an effective admission of defrauding membership.

Nah he just asked y'all to destroy the evidence of his actions and get with him on these new vibes.

Pastor #2

Another famous Pastor is worth 20 million dollars and teach generosity giving he has about 30,000 members. They are both wealthy and live like kings.

But what does the Word of God say about this!!!

CHAPTER NINE

OLD AND NEW TESTAMENT

The reason I chose this topic, or the reason this topic was chosen for me (whichever you prefer) was because recently I heard on a radio broadcast where the host was expressing that the TITHE, which he believed was money, was meant for more than just the pastor, priest etc... Now, to him this was quite a revelation. I sadly, wished I could express to them adequately enough the bigger picture. That the TITHE has NOTHING to do with FINANCES... which is something I hope by now you see for yourself or maybe you don't but I will explain it to you in this book.

The scripture he began with was from Deuteronomy 26:12.

When thou hast made an end of tithing all the tithes of thine increase the third year, which is the year of tithing, and hast given it unto the Levite, the stranger, the fatherless, and the widow, that they may eat within thy gates, and be filled; 13 Then thou shalt say before the Lord thy God, I have brought away the hallowed things out of mine house, and also have given them unto the Levite, and unto the stranger, to the fatherless, and to the widow, according to all thy commandments which thou hast commanded me: I have not transgressed thy commandments, neither have I forgotten them.

It is easy for me to see here that the TITHE that must be given to the Levite, stranger, fatherless, and widow, is not MONEY, but it is AGAPE LOVE, absolute love… which is why it is written, that in doing so (giving the tithe) the COMMANDMENTS (love others, love God) have not been transgressed. Not to MENTION if you love it is impossible to break one of the TEN commandments found in the law. The LAW OF LOVE trumps all.

<u>And yes, if we Love, sometimes the way we show that love is by helping people out financially… but the TITHE that we are to GIVE is the FRUIT OF AN OBEDIENT HEART not ten percent of our check every two weeks</u>.

THE TITHE is the FIRST FRUIT OF THE SPIRIT — And what is the first fruit of the spirit you ask?

Galatians 5:22-23

But the fruit of the Spirit is love, joy, peace, longsuffering, gentleness, goodness, faith, Meekness, temperance: against such there is no law.

And look again at this next definition of the fruit of the spirit.

Ephesians 5:9

(For the fruit of the Spirit is in all goodness and righteousness and truth;)

THIS IS THE TITHE — this is what is meant to be brought into the STOREHOUSE/TEMPLE/YOU — Goodness, Righteousness/Right thinking, Truth, peace, Joy, long-suffering, gentleness, meekness, temperance, and of course AGAPE LOVE! — This is what we are meant to TITHE TO GOD, by TITHING it to others.

DON'T BELIEVE ME YET?

Well let us look at Deut 26 – which clearly explains the TITHE and how we are to come by it. Read carefully, and remember to look deeper at what is being shared, because it may be an allegory of something beautiful you may have missed.

Deuteronomy 26

26 And it shall be, when thou art come in unto the land which the Lord thy God grivet thee for an inheritance, and possesses it, and dwells therein; 2 That thou shalt take of the first of all the fruit of the earth, which thou shalt bring of thy land that the Lord thy God

grivet thee, and shalt put it in a basket, and shalt go unto the place which the Lord thy God shall choose to place his name there.

To TRULY TITHE we must first come to the "LAND" God gave us for an inheritance... and what would that LAND BE?

It is OURSELVES!

Luke 21:19 In your patience possess ye your souls.

We are MEANT TO INHERIT OURSELVES — Psalm 25:13

1 Corinthians 15:47 The first man is of the earth, earthy; the second man is the Lord from heaven.

Think of the EARTH as Temporal AND Heaven as Spiritual. There is the NATURAL MAN (EARTH) and there is the SPIRIT MAN (Heaven).

Now, let us look at it like this... the SPIRIT OF GOD was placed into the HEART OF NATURAL MAN and NATURAL MAN was the land to be inherited. This means, the TWO MUST BECOME ONE... And to have this happen, God brings us into the LAND OF PROMISE which is also called the Kingdom of God. Which we know is Righteousness, Peace and Joy... We are meant to INHERIT eternal LIFE, to know the TRUTH and to be set free from the lies of the world.

We are to be set free to love and to live at peace with others in this world and the world to come.

And WHEN God brings us into this land, when the TRUTH is revealed to us and we begin to lay down our egotistical life for the WILL OF GOD then, and only then, are we meant to take the FIRST FRUIT (peace, joy, love, hope, etc) and GIVE THAT TO THE WORLD.

<u>Yet, the religious will have you to believe it is the TENTH of your literal wages... Jesus clearly tore that idea down when he said...</u>

Matthew 23:23

Woe unto you, scribes and Pharisees, hypocrites! for ye pay tithe of mint and anise and cumin, and have omitted the weightier matters of the law, judgment, mercy, and faith: these ought ye to have done, and not to leave the other undone.

WOE UNTO YOU... FOR WHAT? Why did Jesus say, woe unto you scribes and Pharisees? Well, the reason was simple... that they thought the tithe had to do with their wallets too... and like most

Christians today, they tithe that temporal ten percent and LEAVE OUT the TITHE THAT MATTERS TRULY… judgment, mercy, and faith!

Notice Jesus said… THESE YOU SHOULD HAVE DONE AND NOT LEFT THEM UNDONE!

The TITHE IS NOT MONEY PEOPLE! In the parable of the Pharisee and the Publican praying… the Pharisee bragged about all his Tithes, and all the things he did… while the Publican gave GOD HIS HEART and all of it.

You tell me, which walked away justified and sanctified that day?

I hope this cleared somethings up for you. And I pray that you too bring all your TITHES into the storehouse, so the will of God, which is love, peace, and salvation for all can be found within your heart… so the WINDOWS OF HEAVEN will open up for you and pour blessings upon you but wait there is more!

CHAPTER TEN

OLD AND NEW TESTAMENT

Jesus refocused attention on inward attitudes. He criticized some who went so far as to tithe tiny grains of spice — not because they tithed, but because they neglected the weightier matters of the law (Matt 23:23). He regarded stewardship of finances as an indication of trustworthiness with spiritual things (Luke 16:11), which were more important (Matt 6:19-20).

Nowhere does the New Testament require Christians to tithe in the sense of giving 10 percent, but it does reiterate many things associated with tithing: those who minister are entitled to receive support (1 Cur 9:14); the poor and needy should be cared for (1 Cor 16:1; Gal 2:10); those who give can trust God, as the source of all that is given (2 Cor 9:10), to supply their needs (2 Cor 9:8; Philippians 4:19); and giving should be done joyously (2 Cor 9:7).

The New Testament directs that taxes be paid to the state (Romans 13:6-7), which replaced Israel's theocracy. Paul's vocabulary and teaching suggest that giving is voluntary and that there is no set percentage. Following the example of Christ, who gave even his life (2 Cor 8:9), we should cheerfully give as much as we have decided (2 Cor 9:7) based on how much the Lord has prospered us (1 Cor 16:2), knowing that we reap in proportion to what we sow (2 Cor 9:6) and that we will ultimately give account for our deeds (Romans 14:12).

A tithe is really an Old Testament term. It was the gifts that the Israelites were required to, really the tax that they were required to pay. Nowadays we generally use it as just a way of saying give 10% of your income to the church. There's nothing in the New Testament, in the sort of new covenant understanding of what it means to be God's people, that encourages us to think that we're required to give 10% of our income to the church.

In many ways the standards of the New Testament are a lot stricter in some ways, or a lot loftier, let's put it that way. So we're required to give generously, to give sacrificially, to see the relief of the poor, the support of the ministry, the spread of the gospel through all nations. There may be some people for whom giving 10% is unwise. There are probably many people in America for whom giving 10% would be actually pretty easy, and in fact it wouldn't really be sacrificial or generous.

NOW Does Tithing Apply to Christians Today?

The reason why tithing is an important theme for Christians is because it really is a symbol of how God calls us to live our lives as stewards rather than owners.

I come from a legalistic background where I used to be afraid not to tithe, or I used to be proud of tithing. My fear was if I didn't tithe, my tires would fall off my car or God would take it out of my hide and cause me to die or have an accident. My arrogance was if I tithe then God had to bless me with prosperity. But really to reflect upon tithing in the context of the gospel, what we begin to demonstrate or see is this ... that the more the law of God is transformed by the GRACE (God Riches at Christ Expense) of God in our lives, we move from a sense of duty to a sense of delight. This is why really in the New Testament you don't hear a whole lot about tithing, not because believers are not expected to give, they're just expected to be a lot more generous because of the fullness of the work of Jesus that we celebrate.

Paul demonstrated this in writing to believers in Corinth and reflecting upon a group of very poor Christians in Thessalonica. And he wrote to believers in Corinth because he was trying to generate their interest in caring for a ministry to the poor believers in Jerusalem.

And here's the way he motivated them, said, "We want you to know about the grace that came to believers in Macedonia, who, out of their extreme poverty and suffering, did not do as we expected. They gave themselves to the Lord, and then they asked us for the privilege of sharing in this offering."

Now what Paul does there is this, he doesn't shame believers in Corinth into tithing. He simply says, here's what the Gospel does when it grabs hold of your heart. You don't think just in terms of giving the excess, but you're showing up in God's story, which is a story of redemption and restoration. A story that frees me from defining my life in terms of what I own, rather who owns me, which is Jesus.

So in many ways, tithing is kind of the entrance level into a life of grace. The more the grace of the gospel captures my heart, the less I'm going to ask, "How much do I have to give," but more, "How can I live more fully mission ally, generously to the glory of God," because of the lavish love, the great generosity, God's lavished upon me in Jesus.

Does All of My Tithe Have to Go to the Church?

This is another question that is asked by Christians?

If I were to get to summarize it in a nutshell, I would say please do whatever you can to be a part of a church where you would be comfortable giving 100% of your offering to that church. I want to start with that, but let me unpack that. I think the word tithe is not so helpful in discussing Christian giving anymore. If we go and look at what happened under the Old Covenant in the Old Testament, a godly Hebrew man would've given anywhere from 30% to 35% of his income to the support of the temple, the support of the poor, the support of the priests. I mean, it was a pretty hefty tax, if you will, to be part of the Kingdom of God under the Old Testament.

Well, when you get to the New Testament, the command to tithe is not there. What it's been replaced by is what I would call grace-giving, which is exactly what Paul says in Second Corinthians eight. He refers to giving as an act of grace. You go to Second Corinthians nine and he talks about cheerful giving. And there are so many other places in the gospels. I think Luke 12, where you get this idea that because God has given us so much, we should be willing to give everything over to others.

So in the New Testament, you have this idea of grace giving. Not only that, but in the New Testament you have this idea that ground zero for Christian ministry is the church, Acts 1A. You see this great commission at work to bring the Gospel to Jerusalem and Judea and Sumerian into all the ends of the earth. And then what do you see? The Gospel is planted, churches sprout up, and then churches now bear the responsibility of planting the gospel throughout the world. So the church is ground zero for Christian ministry.

So to someone who comes to me and says hey, do I have to give all of my tithes to the church, what I want to say is what I want you to do is be a part of a church that you see is so faithful to the Bible, has a heart for the nations, has elders who are really worthy of double honor, and I want you to have the heart to give everything to that church. But having said that, I think you're absolutely free to give to Godly para-church ministries that are serving the Lord, especially ones that you may be personally involved in or personally excited about. You're free to give to those ministries.

So I guess I'm not directly answering the question. We give out of grace because we love the Lord. We give to a church that is doing the work of the Lord. And above and beyond that, we are absolutely free to give to other good, solid ministries.

CHAPTER ELEVEN

WHAT IS TITHING?

Let us make it more clearer
Let's start by looking at a few tithing definitions:
Wikipedia defines the tithe:
"A tithe (/taɪð/; from Old English: teogoþa "tenth") is a one-tenth part of something, paid as a contribution to a religious organization or compulsory tax to government. Today, tithes are normally voluntary and paid in cash, cheques, or stocks, whereas historically tithes were required and paid in kind, such as agricultural products."

And Webster's Dictionary defines tithe like this:
"a tenth part of something paid as a voluntary contribution or as a tax especially for the support of a religious establishment"

What the Bible says about tithing

If you search for the word tithing in the Bible (and tithe), you will find about 14 scriptures mentioning it (depending on which version you are using).

For the sake of brevity, I won't list them all here, but these are a few of the most popular Bible verses about tithing:

The first mention of tithing in the Bible

"Then Melchizedek king of Salem brought out bread and wine. He was priest of God Most High, and he blessed Abram, saying, "Blessed be Abram by God Most High, Creator of heaven and earth. And praise be to God Most High, who delivered your enemies into your hand." Then Abram gave him a tenth of everything." – Gen 14:18-20 NIV

The most popular Tithing scripture

"Bring the whole tithe into the storehouse, so that there may be food in My house, and test Me now in this," says the LORD of hosts, "if I will not open for you the windows of heaven and pour out for you a blessing until it overflows."

Mal 3:10 NASB

The New Testament scripture on tithing

So, what does the new testament say about tithing? Not a lot, but Jesus said this in Luke...

"But woe to you Pharisees! For you pay tithe of mint and rue and every kind of garden herb, and yet disregard justice and the love of God; but these are the things you should have done without neglecting the others." – Luke 11:42 NASB

It is pretty clear from all the Bible verses on money and tithing (let alone the three above), that tithing is a Biblical idea. Now, what it means for us today is a hotly debated topic that we will explore in a bit.

Tithing Isn't a Means of Salvation

This is incredibly important to understand. Our salvation is based on Jesus' finished work on the cross, not on works.

You can't earn your way to Heaven by giving, and you won't be excluded from Heaven by your lack of tithing.

"For it is by grace you have been saved, through faith—and this not from yourselves, it is the gift of God— not by works, so that no one can boast." –Ephesians 2:8-9 (NIV)

Out of our Faith, our good works manifest. So, in my opinion, if someone truly understands how great of a gift they have been given, they will expend a lot of energy giving back.

CHAPTER TWELVE

THE PRINCIPLES OF TITHING

Hebrews 7:1-10
New International Version
Melchizedek the Priest

7 This Melchizedek was king of Salem and priest of God Most High. He met Abraham returning from the defeat of the kings and blessed him, and Abraham gave him a tenth of everything. First, the name Melchizedek means "king of righteousness"; then also, "king of Salem" means "king of peace." ³Without father or mother, without genealogy, without beginning of days or end of life, resembling the Son of God, he remains a priest forever.

⁴Just think how great he was: Even the patriarch Abraham gave him a tenth of the plunder! ⁵Now the law requires the descendants of Levi who become priests to collect a tenth from the people—that is, from their fellow Israelites—even though they also are descended from Abraham. ⁶This man, however, did not trace his descent from Levi, yet he collected a tenth from Abraham and blessed him who had the promises. ⁷And without doubt the lesser is blessed by the greater. ⁸In the one case, the tenth is collected by people who die; but in the other case, by him who is declared to be living. ⁹One might

even say that Levi, who collects the tenth, paid the tenth through Abraham, ¹⁰because when Melchizedek met Abraham, Levi was still in the body of his ancestor.

Hebrews 7:1-10

King James Version

7 For this Melchisedec, king of Salem, priest of the highest God, who met Abraham returning from the slaughter of the kings, and blessed him;

²To whom also Abraham gave a tenth part of all; first being by interpretation King of righteousness, and after that also King of Salem, which is, King of peace;

³Without father, without mother, without descent, having neither beginning of days, nor end of life; but made like unto the Son of God; abided a priest continually.

⁴Now consider how great this man was, unto whom even the patriarch Abraham gave the tenth of the spoils.

⁵And verily they that are of the sons of Levi, who receive the office of the priesthood, have a commandment to take tithes of the people according to the law, that is, of their brethren, though they come out of the loins of Abraham:

⁶But he whose descent is not counted from them received tithes of Abraham, and blessed him that had the promises.

⁷And without all contradiction the less is blessed of the better.

⁸And here men that die receive tithes; but there he received them, of whom it is witnessed that he lived.

⁹And as I may so say, Levi also, who received tithes, payed tithes in Abraham.

¹⁰For he was yet in the loins of his father, when Melchisedec met him.

The entire chapter here is devoted to showing how Jesus is the fulfillment of all the types and shadows embodied in Melchisedec it gives special attention to the fact that Abraham tithed to Melchizedek who was either Jesus Christ himself or a representation of Christ. Plus, all this occurred 430 years before the Mosaic Law.

It teaches 3 simple and beautiful things about God's design for tithing and the central place of tithing in God's economy.

THITHING IS AN ETERNAL PRINCIPLE

Many say tithing is just for the old testament, but it is not. God simply allowed the Levites, during the time of the Mosaic Law, to exercise it in their behalf because they had no inheranitence.

So, let's go back to the first mention of Melchizedec;

Genesis 14:18-20 18 And Melchizedek king of Salem brought forth bread and wine: and he was the priest of the highest God. 19 And he blessed him, and said, Blessed be Abram of the highest God, possessor of heaven and earth: 20 And blessed be the highest God, which hath delivered thine enemies into thy hand. And he gave him tithes of all.

430 years before tithing was part of the Mosaic Law, Abraham tithe to Melchizedek. According to the book of Galatian, Abraham is our spiritual father and Melchizedek is a type of Jesus Christ. Some prominent Bible teachers think he might even have been Jesus Christ Himself.

We also know Melchizedek is a type of Christ because because Hebrews 5:9-10 says so:

Hebrews 5:9-10 KJV

and being made perfect, he became the author of eternal salvation unto all them that obey him; called of God a high priest after the order of Melchisedec.

Our text presents a full portrait of Melchizedek which underscores the full depth and meaning of the book of Hebrews, because it tells us the full story of Melchizedek and the present day reasons and the meaning of the tithe.

Notice his title from Hebrews 7:2

Hebrews 7:2 King James Version 2

To whom also Abraham gave a tenth part of all; first being by interpretation King of righteousness (same as justice), and after that also King of Salem, which is, King of peace; He is made like unto the Son of God, so that means he is a type of Christ, he is fulfilled in Jesus.

Notice Hebrews 7;3.

Hebrews 7:3 King James Version (KJV) 3 Without father, without mother, without descent, having neither beginning of days, nor end of life; but made like unto the Son of God; abideth a priest continually. King James Version (KJV)

Notice Hebrews 7:3 Underscore the object of the apostle in using Melzchidek as an example is to vindicate the fact that Jesus is our High Priest. Every priest had to vindicate his genology. His ancestry had to be verified. Before he could be excepted as a priest, he had to prove that he was of the tribe of Levi the son of Aaron (see Ezra 2:61-63).

Ezra 2:61-63 [61]And from among the priests: The descendants of Obadiah, Hakes and Barilla (a man who had married a daughter of Barilla the Gileadean and was called by that name). [62]These searched for their family records, but they could not find them and so were excluded from the priesthood as unclean. [63]The governor ordered them not to eat any of the most sacred food until there was a priest ministering with the Uri and Thomism.

They heat scrupulous records. When that ancestry could not be traced to Aaron. They were for priesthood purposes, said to be without father or mother. But Jesus was of the tribe of Judah not of Levi. So, in this Sense Christ was without father or mother.

But Paul is reminding them there is a precedence for this. This is not the first time a non-Levite served God as a high priest —- Melchizedek did.

This act of tithe-giving signified that Abraham recognized him as a superior – even to himself.

His office was priest of the Highest GOD- he had intimate access to the DIVINE presence.

He offered sacrifices to GOD.

His residence was in Salem meaning "KING OF PEACE', CHRIST IS THE PRIENCE OF PEACE. So, if Melchezdek a Non-Levite, a type of CHRIST, could be a priest, much more can Jesus Christ be a priest who is far greater. I've said all this to show you that tithing is an eternal principle.

Hebrews 7-8 is a most remarkable verse. According to this verse, Jesus receives the tithe in heaven. When you write your tithe check, you may think you are giving it to your local church, but in a very real and spiritual sense, true tithers have their money received by the Lord Jesus Himself.

Tithing is an eternal principal, it was begun before the law, continued during the law and continues today, after the law.

CHAPTER THIRTEEN

TITHING IS A PERFECTED PRINCIPAL

The whole emphases of Hebrews are to show how Jesus perfected the Mosaic system. He did not do away with the sacrificial system, he perfected it.

Hebrews 7:11

King James Version

¹¹ If therefore perfection were by the Levitical priesthood, (for under it the people received the law,) what further need was there that another priest should rise after the order of Melchisedec, and not be called after the order of Aaron?

He perfected it by one sacrifice once and for all.

How is the tithe perfected? Christ can't give it for us?

Can we make a once for all offering? NO.

Then how is the tithe perfected. We perfect the tithe when we give the tithe to Jesus because we love Him not because we are forced to just as He gave His life for us because He loved us.

God wants us to love Him and trust Him and serve Him and there is no better way than to trust Him than with earthly mammon. Money represents your life and when you honor God with the tithe, you honor Him with your very life.

The tithe is only a begging. It is a start; we can do nothing less. It is the point from which we can tell how serious we are about honoring God.

As one writer said "if we are not willing to give a tithe, then we need not pretend we are going to serve Him in all his commands. We need not act as if He is lord of our lives. We need not tell people that we have submitted ourselves to Him if we are not willing to come up to that bare minimum of tithing which the Jew under the Law was commanded to do."

CHAPTER FOURTEEN

PRINCIPLE NUMBER 2

Principle number 2 has to do with our motives for giving. We should give because we love God and want to obey GOD, PERIOD. We should not give mechanilly because we want to get something in return. You simply give because you love JESUS. Lets just keep it simple. Why do I tithe? Why do I give offerings? Because I love Jesus. Tithing is a matter of the Spirit not the heart because the heart is part of the mind and the Spirit is part of the born-again nature.

CHAPTER FIFTEEN

TITHING IS A BLESSSED PRINCIPLE

The tithe is perfected also in that God gives back to us what we give.

Proverbs 11:24

"There is that scattereth, and yet increaseth; and **there is** that withholdeth more than is meet, but **it tendeth** to poverty.

Malachi 3:10-15 King James Version (KJV) 10 Bring ye all the tithes into the storehouse, that there may be meat in mine house, and prove me now herewith, saith the Lord of hosts, if I will not open you the windows of heaven, and pour you out a blessing, that there shall not be room enough to receive it.

You the Technology of God, the temple of God is the "STOREHOUSE".

Luke 6:38

King James Version

[38] Give, and it shall be given unto you; good measure, pressed down, and shaken together, and running over, shall men give into your bosom. For with the same measure that ye mete withal it shall be measured to you again.

This is a prinicipal of life. The whole physical world operates this way. If we give our time to an employer. We receive money in exchange. Farmers give their toil to the earth and then receive harvest. That is the law of seedtime and harvest.

To say you can not afford to tithe is dangerous.

As one said, "the most dangerous thing in all the earth is to contradict one of the principal of GOD for our lives." The truth is, you can not afford not to tithe.

CHAPTER SIXTEEN

THE TEN PRINCIPLES OF TITHING

So far in this series I have looked at the disciple's relationship to money from a number of angles. Now it's time to consider tithing, which simply means giving a tenth of our income to God and his kingdom work.

An Acknowledgement of God's Authority over our Lives and Wealth tithing is a practice that goes all the way back to Genesis, which is first mentioned when Abraham gave a tenth of the spoils of war to Melchizedek, a priest-king of Jerusalem, who many believe was at least a type of Christ. With God's help, Abraham had just defeated a coalition of pagan kings to rescue his nephew, Lot, and his family.

Then Melchizedek king of Salem brought out bread and wine. He was priest of God Most High, 19 and he blessed Abram, saying, "Blessed be Abram by God Most High, Creator of heaven and earth. 20 And blessed be God Most High, who delivered your enemies into your hand." Then Abram gave him a tenth of everything. Genesis 14:18-20 (NIV)

Tithing was a common practice in that day and long predated the giving of the Law to Moses, at which time tithing became part of the legal code of Israel. In Abraham's case, he was tithing to a person, who was greater than he, as a way of acknowledging that he was under his authority and blessing, which brings us to our first tithing principles.

Principle One: Tithing shows that we acknowledge God's authority over our lives and finances.

Principle Two: Tithing reveals that we believe that God is our Provider. It is from him all blessings flow, and to him we return a tenth.

A tithe of everything from the land, whether grain from the soil or fruit from the trees, belongs to the LORD; it is holy to the LORD. Leviticus 27:30 (NIV)

If we accept that the tithe belongs to God, then those who withhold giving the tithe are actually robbing God, keeping for themselves what is rightfully God's.

"Will a man rob God? Yet you rob me. "But you ask, 'How do we rob you?' "In tithes and offerings. 9 You are under a curse—the whole nation of you—because you are robbing me. Malachi 3:8-9 (NIV)

Those who robbed God in this manner brought upon themselves a curse or judgment. Instead of experiencing God's supernatural provision, they would experience being robbed themselves by the "devourer."

A GATEWAY TO BLESSING

Bring the whole tithe into the storehouse, that there may be food in my house. Test me in this," says the LORD Almighty, "and see if I will not throw open the floodgates of heaven and pour out so much blessing that you will not have room enough for it. 11 I will prevent pests from devouring your crops, and the vines in your fields will not cast their fruit," says the LORD Almighty. Malachi 3:10-11 (NIV)

Principle Three: Giving to God what is his already opens the door to God's returning immense blessings to us. It is an amazing thing that God rewards us for doing our duty.

It is not that we give to get. Rather, we give because we believe that God, our Provider, will supply well beyond our needs as we sacrificially give to him and his kingdom. Tithing often takes money that we feel we need. When we choose to give it to God, he knows what we need and makes provision for his people. There are countless stories of people who began to tithe by faith, only to see God surprise them with unexpected and unforeseen provisions. God delights in honoring the faith of his people in this way.

A Means of Provision for those who THE LEVITES Serve on a Full-time Basis.

I give to the Levites all the tithes in Israel as their inheritance in return for the work they do while serving at the Tent of Meeting. Numbers 18:21 (NIV)

(2) Under the Law of Moses, the tithe supported God's appointed representatives, the Levites and priests, who served God in the stead of the entire nation.

(3) The tithe enabled them to serve Undistractedly

Without worry of how they would be able to provide for their own families.

If the people of Israel tithed, the priests and Levites were able to perform their assigned duties.

If the people failed to tithe, the work of God suffered because the workers had to use other means to stay alive and make ends meet.

PORTIONS OF THE LEVITES

I also learned that the portions assigned to the Levites had not been given to them, and that all the Levites and singers responsible for the service had gone back to their own fields.
Nehemiah 13:10 (NIV)

CHAPTER TITHING CHURCH AND JOB

Today, when people tithe to the local church (the New Covenant version of the Old Covenant "storehouse").

it enables called servants of God to serve without encumbrance in their service to the Lord.

SECULAR JOBS

Secular jobs take enormous amounts of time, which subtract from what is available for the Lord's work of study, prayer, counseling, visitation, sharing the Gospel, disciple making, and whatever else might present itself during a day to a pastor or other full-time church leader.

(1) It is my conviction that the number one priority for church spending is to support the five-fold ministry – apostles, prophets, evangelists, pastors, and teachers, because the work of the kingdom depends on their having the means and ability to serve.

CHAPTER EIGHTEEN

PROVIDING FOR THOSE IN NEED

A Provision for the Poor and the Marginalized
Every three years a special tithe was collected in Israel, which was specifically used for helping not only the Levites, but also foreigners, widows, and orphans – the poor who cannot provide adequately for themselves.

(3) Buildings and such come in a distant third.

CHAPTER NINETEEN

PRINCIPLE FIVE LOCAL CHURCHES

Local churches are able to help the poor and those facing unexpected hardships by using the tithe in conjunction with other special offerings.

When you have finished setting aside a tenth of all your produce in the third year, the year of the tithe, you shall give it to the Levite, the alien, the fatherless and the widow, so that they may eat in your towns and be satisfied. Deuteronomy 26:12 (NIV)

The Tithe in the New Covenant

Woe to you Pharisees, because you give God a tenth of your mint, rue and all other kinds of garden herbs, but you neglect justice and the love of God. You should have practiced the latter without leaving the former undone. Luke 11:42 (NIV)

There is not a lot written about the tithe in the New Testament. Jesus told the Pharisees that they were both to tithe and keep the more important aspects of the Law.

This would have been the perfect place for him to throw out the tithe as he did with ceremonial washing and other dietary laws, but he did not.

CHAPTER TWENTY

TITHE IS BUILT INTO THE FRAMEWORK OF HUMANITY

The tithe is outside the jurisdiction of the Law and is actually built into the framework of humanity, going back to Genesis and creation itself.

One of the ideas advanced by those who teach that tithing is required under the New Testament is the belief that tithing is an eternal principle.

Those who teach that tithing is an eternal principle make appeal to two texts which predate the giving of the Law through Moses: (1) the tree of the knowledge of good and evil in the garden of Eden, and (2) Abraham's tithe to Mechisedek.

First, the belief that the tree of the knowledge of good and evil was Adam's tithe is a pervasive doctrine, mainly within Word of Faith theology, even though there is not a single text in all of scripture that hints to such a notion. This teaching is based solely on the private revelation of men, and it is not taught anywhere within the pages of scripture.

Well then, what about Abraham's tithe to Melchizedek?

In Genesis 14, we read of the battle of the Kings. There were four Kings: King Amraphel of Babylonia, King Arioch of Ellasar, King Kedorlaomer of Elam, and King Tidal of Goiim.

These four Kings went to battle against five other Kings

The five other Kings were: King Bera of Sodom, King Birsha of Gomorrah, King Shinab of Admah, King Shemeber of Zeboiim, and the king of Bela (aka Zoar).

Now the second group of kings (the five Kings), had came together in the Siddim Valley, which is the valley of the Dead Sea. They had been under the rule of King Kedorlaomer who is mentioned in the list of the first 4 Kings above.

The five Kings who joined forces had been his subjects for 12 years and in the 13th year they rebelled against him. Notice that two of the five Kings who were subjects to Kedorlaomer, were the King of Sodom and the King of Gomorrah.

These five Kings fought against the four Kings. In verses 10-16 we read the following:

As it happened, the valley of the Dead Sea was filled with tar pits. And as the army of the kings of Sodom and Gomorrah fled, some fell into the tar pits, while the rest escaped into the mountains. The victorious invaders then plundered Sodom and Gomorrah and headed for home, taking with them all the spoils of war and the food supplies. They also captured Lot — Abram's Newphew who lived in Sodom—and carried off everything he owned. But one of Lot's men escaped and reported everything to Abram the Hebrew, who was living near the oak grove belonging to Mamre the Amorite. Mamre and his relatives, Eshcol and Aner, were Abram's allies. When Abram heard that his nephew Lot had been captured, he mobilized the 318 trained men who had been born into his household. Then he pursued Kedorlaomer's army until he caught up with them at Dan. There he divided his men and attacked during the night. Kedorlaomer's army fled, but Abram chased them as far as Hobah, north of Damascus. Abram recovered all the goods that had been taken, and he brought back his nephew Lot with his possessions and all the women and other captives. ~ Genesis 14:10-16 (The New Living Translation)

Notice that verse 16 says, "Abram recovered all the goods that had been taken…"

These "goods" are the specific contents, from which Abraham gave a tenth to Melchizedek (v. 17-20).

Abraham did not give Melchizedek a tenth of his own personal wealth. In fact, there is no record that Abraham gave Melchizedek anything from his personal possessions. Abraham gave only that which was from the spoils of war to Melchizedek.

According to Russell Earl Kelly (a theologian on the topic of tithing) Abraham's tithe to Melchizedek was an ancient Arab custom.

Under the Arab custom, the spoil-tithe tax was ten percent of the spoil. However, under the Mosaic Law, the spoil-tithe tax which came from the spoils of war was only one percent and was given to the Levites and (one tenth) of that (one percent) was given to the priests.

The required tithe tax from the spoil of war under the Law of Moses was actually LESS than what Abraham gave to Melchizedek.

Now, most people usually stop at Abraham paying tithes to Melchizedek, but if we continue reading, we find that Abraham did not keep any of the spoils of war for himself, but returned them to their rightful owner: The King of Sodom!

The king of Sodom said to Abram, "Give back my people who were captured. But you may keep for yourself all the goods you have recovered." Abram replied to the king of Sodom, "I solemnly swear to the Lord, God Highest, Creator of heaven and earth, that I will not take so much as a single thread or sandal thong from that what belongs to you. Otherwise you might say, 'I am the one who made Abram rich.' I will accept only what my young warriors have already eaten, and I request that you give a fair share of the goods to my allies —Aner, Eshcol, and Mamre." ~ Genesis 14:21-24

Notice that Abraham acknowledges that the goods from which he gave a tenth to Melchizedek, actually belonged to the King of Sodom. If Abraham's tithe is proof of an eternal principle, then it is an eternal principle to tithe from the goods which belong to another, and not from that which belongs to you.

There is no record in scripture that Abraham ever gave a tenth of his personal wealth. Abraham's tithe was a one-time gift to King Melchizedek, and the contents of that tithe was the spoils of war. The rest (nearly 90%), Abraham returned to its rightful owner, the King of Sodom.

There is absolutely nothing in the context of Genesis 14 which would lead the careful reader to come to the conclusion that Abraham's tithe from the spoils of war establishes tithing is an eternal principle. It simply isn't there!

Yes, According to 2 sources.

CHAPTER TWENTY ONE

TITHING IS AN ETERNAL PRINCPLE

Tithing is an eternal principle. It was begun before the Law, continued during the Law, and continues today, after the Law.

2) Tithing is a perfected principle.

The whole emphasis of Hebrews is to show how Jesus perfected the Mosaic system. He did not do away with the sacrificial system. He perfected it.

One of the ideas advanced by those who teach that tithing is required under the New Testament is the belief that tithing is an eternal principle.

The only other place tithing is mentioned in the New Testament Is in the the Letter to the Hebrews, where the author makes a case for Jesus' superiority over the Aaronic priesthood.

See how great this man was to whom Abraham the patriarch gave a tenth of the spoils! 5 And those descendants of Levi who receive the priestly office have a commandment in the law to take tithes from the people, that is, from their brothers, though these also are descended from Abraham. 6 But this man who does not have his descent from them received tithes from Abraham and blessed him who had the promises. 7 It is beyond dispute that the inferior is blessed by the superior. 8 In the one case tithes are received by mortal men, but in the other case, by one of whom it is testified that he lives. 9 One might even say that Levi himself, who receives tithes, paid tithes through Abraham, 10 for he was still in the loins of his ancestor when Melchizedek met him. Hebrews 7:4-10 (ESV)

THE LESSER SUPPORTS THE GREATER

In this case, the tithe once again shows how the lesser supports the greater. It's a matter of authority and blessing and recognizing the need to support the five-fold ministry.

Some argue that the tithe is "legalistic" and was done away with in the New Covenant. To these, I point out that Jesus never did away with God's authority over and ownership of our finances. He clearly stated that a true disciple of "GENEROSITY" is one who serves God, not money. In fact, our Lord said that a disciple is one who gives up everything for the sake of the kingdom of God.

So then, none of you can be My disciple who does not give up all his own possessions. Luke 14:33.

The rich young ruler was offered the opportunity to sell all and become part of Jesus' traveling band of disciples. What an opportunity and honor! Jesus still holds the power to call each and everyone of his followers to the same high standard with regard to money.

PRINCIPLE TWO GOD DOES NOT ASK LESS OF US

If God required at least a tenth from his Old Covenant saints, is it probable, or even conceivable, that he would ask less of us?

The only legitimate way to do away with the tithe is to move up to the New Covenant standard of giving everything.

TITHING IS A MATTER OF THE SPIRIT NOT THE HEART

Over the years, I have known some who objected to tithing because they were selfish and wanted to hold on to their finances for themselves. Others refuse to be limited by the tithe and give much more. Ultimately tithing and all giving is a matter of the spirit not heart. If it is not done willingly, it is not worth a whole lot, at least in terms of heavenly reward.

PRINCIPAL TWENTY -THREE SHOULD NOT BE APPROACHED LEGALISTICALLY

Tithing should not be approached legalistically. It is something we do by faith because we believe it is the right thing to do and because we trust that God is our provider. If we give willingly and cheerfully, God will see it and return a blessing.

And God is able to make all grace abound to you, so that in all things at all times, having all that you need, you will abound in every good work. 2 Corinthians 9:8 (NIV)

God asks some disciples to give all their money and resources to him, as he did with the rich young ruler. For the rest of us, as we consider how God would want us to give toward his kingdom, ten percent is a great place to start when you look at Thessilonia 5:23 man consist of spirit, soul and body the spirit consist os 60% of the man which is spiritual part which is born again, the soul consist of 60% which is still carnal part of the man and the body consist of 10% which is the flesh part of the man. It is this 10% which is the natural part which is still lost and unsaved that does not understand tithing.

PRINCIPLE TWENTY-FOUR TITHING SHOULD BE A MINIMUM

I believe we should consider it a minimum, a "no brainer," an automatic category in our budget. Giving beyond the tithe is an opportunity to listen to the Spirit of God for his direction in our giving. This kind of giving is sometimes called making "offerings." It is an act of obedience to the Spirit, a spiritual sacrifice that pleases God, and is a function of our faith in God and the generosity of our hearts. We learn the art of generous giving by starting with the tithe and getting saved by grace and progressing beyond.

I have tithed for years out of conviction and faith. I cannot imagine doing otherwise. I know many others who have done the same. In fact, I know of no one who has tithed regularly who does not agree that God abundantly "GRACE" (GOD RICHES

AT CHRIST EXPENSE) supplies all our needs. The work of the kingdom somewhat depends on the generosity of the people of God. Let's be faithful in giving.

If you have never GIVEN GENEROUSLY, give it a try. God promises to faithfully bless you.

"Should people cheat God? Yet you have cheated me! "But you ask, 'What do you mean? When did we ever cheat you?' "You have cheated me of the tithes and offerings due to me. 9 You are under a curse, for your whole nation has been cheating me. 10 Bring all the tithes into the storehouse so there will be enough food in my Temple (YOU ARE THE TEMPLE OF GOD. You give out of yourself, out of the work you do. If you do," says the LORD of Heaven's Armies, "I will open the windows of heaven for you. I will pour out a blessing so great you won't have enough room to take it in! Try it! Put me to the test! Malachi 3:8-10 (NLT)

Imagine! God wants us to test him in this matter! Have you exercised your faith by giving to God money you think you need to make ends meet, because you acknowledge that he is your supplier and can somehow make up the difference and more? It's time to get started. You may be cheating yourself out of an amazing blessing!

PRINCIPLE TWENTY-FIVE TITHING OPENS UP BLESSINGS

Once you find out that tithing opens up blessings, you will be ready to ask God, "How much do you want me to give beyond the tithe?" remember tithing is a principle a matter of the spirit. Then you will be ready for a really exciting ride!

One thing is for sure, if we give little, we will reap a small blessing. If that is what you want, have at it.

Remember this—a farmer who plants only a few seeds will get a small crop. But the one who plants generously will get a generous crop. You must each decide in your spirit how much to give. And don't give reluctantly or in response to pressure. "For God loves a person who gives cheerfully." And God will generously provide all you need. Then you will always have everything you need and plenty left over to share with others.

2 Corinthians 9:6-8

I rather think we all want more than that. Try tithing. You'll like it.

PRINCIPALS TWENTY-SIX TITHING IS ABOUT OBEDIENCE

Obedience is the first law of heaven Without it the elements could not be controlled. Without it there could be no union or order, and chaos and confusion would prevail." Order is not the first law of Heaven; obedience is the first law of Heaven, and order is the result." Obedience brings harmony and order to all God's creations. The entire universe teaches us that there is divine law governing all things, that a supreme intelligence controls to the remotest parts of space, as far as man is able to discern the universe. Because of this obedience to law, there is perfect order and harmony."

OBEDIENCE GOVERNS AND DITATES THE ORDER OF CREATION

Obedience governs and dictates the Order of Creation. Some may find it easy to accept that obedience governs the Order of Creation, but still question whether obedience also dictates or requires that it must be so. In the universe where in every kingdom natural law prevails in perfect order and harmony. it is inconsistent to believe that the kingdom of God-the greatest of all kingdoms-is not subject to the same law of obedience and order, as all else in the universe."

WHAT IS THE LAW OF OBEDIENCE?

Bible Verses About Obedience- Obedience to God's commands is the true sign of your love for God, and the only way you can know if you are obeying God is by knowing his Word. Discover the top Bible verses about obedience and submitting to God's will.

Exodus 19:5

5 Now if you obey me fully and keep my covenant, then out of all nations you will be my treasured possession. Although the whole earth is mine,

Deuteronomy 11:1

1 Love the LORD your God and keep his requirements, his decrees, his laws and his commands always.

John 15:9

9 "As the Father has loved me, so have I loved you. Now remain in my love.

2 Corinthians 10:5

5 We demolish arguments and every pretension that sets itself up against the knowledge of God, and we take captive every thought to make it obedient to Christ.

Ephesians 6:1-3

1 Children, obey your parents in the Lord, for this is right. 2 "Honor your father and mother"—which is the first commandment with a promise— 3 "so that it may go well with you and that you may enjoy long life on the earth."

Revelation 14:12

12 This calls for patient endurance on the part of the people of God who keep his commands and remain faithful to Jesus.

Romans 1:5

5 Through him we received grace and apostleship to call all the Gentiles to the obedience that comes from faith for his name's sake.

Hebrews 13:17

17 Have confidence in your leaders and submit to their authority, because they keep watch over you as those who must give an account. Do this so that their work will be a joy, not a burden, for that would be of no benefit to you.

John 15:14

14 You are my friends if you do what I command.

John 14:15

15 "If you love me, keep my commands.

2 John 1:6

6 And this is love: that we walk in obedience to his commands. As you have heard from the beginning, his command is that you walk in love.

Joshua 5:6

The Israelites had moved about in the wilderness forty years until all the men who were of military age when they left Egypt had died, since they had not obeyed the LORD. For the LORD had sworn to them that they would not see the land he had solemnly promised their ancestors to give us, a land flowing with milk and honey.

Romans 2:6-8

6 God "will repay each person according to what they have done." 7 To those who by persistence in doing good seek glory, honor and immortality, he will give eternal life. 8 But for those who are self-seeking and who reject the truth and follow evil, there will be wrath and anger.

Luke 11:28

28 He replied, "Blessed rather are those who hear the word of God and obey it."

Colossians 3:22

Chapter Parallel Compare

22 Slaves, obey your earthly masters in everything; and do it, not only when their eye is on you and to curry their favor, but with sincerity of heart and reverence for the Lord.

Romans 5:19

19 For just as through the disobedience of the one man the many were made sinners, so also through the obedience of the one man the many will be made righteous.

1 Peter 1:14

14 As obedient children, do not conform to the evil desires you had when you lived in ignorance.

James 1:25

25 But whoever looks intently into the perfect law that gives freedom, and continues in it—not forgetting what they have heard, but doing it—they will be blessed in what they do.

So what is the law of obedience? "There is a law, irrevocably decreed in heaven before the foundations of this world, upon which all blessings are predicated–And when we obtain any blessing from God, it is by obedience to that law upon which it is predicated." The relationship between the law of obedience and the Order of Creation can be illustrated by the order or sequence of resurrection.

"The order of resurrection is from most righteous to most wicked. Those who are celestial will come forth before those who are terrestrial, and so forth." Order in the resurrection is determined by obedience to gospel law. The most righteous man was first, the most wicked shall be the last; Christ was first, the sons of perdition shall be last." 9

So why do the most righteous get to be resurrected first? Because they earned that privilege through their obedience to law. It has been irrevocably decreed, so that even God himself cannot alter the order. This decree came "before the foundations of this world." The same law of obedience dictates that in the spirit creation, the most obedient intelligences were privileged to be born first. ORDER TO CREATION

Now that we understand why there is an order to creation in the Order of Creation, the door to even greater learning is opened to us.

OBEDIENCE IS THE FIRST LAW OF HEAVEN

"Obedience is the first law of heaven, the cornerstone upon which all righteousness and progression rest. It consists in compliance with divine law, in conformity to the mind and will of Deity, in complete subjection to God and his commands."

OBEDIENCE IS AN ACT OF WORSHIP

Obedience Is an Act of Worship "Just tell me what to do and I will do it, Lord. As long as I live I'll wholeheartedly obey" (Psalm 119:33-34 TLB). God smiles when we obey him wholeheartedly. That means doing whatever God asks without reservation or hesitation.

"Just tell me what to do and I will do it, Lord. As long as I live I'll wholeheartedly obey" (Psalm 119:33-34 TLB).

God smiles when we obey him wholeheartedly. That means doing whatever God asks without reservation or hesitation. You don't procrastinate and say, "I'll pray about it." You do it without delay. Every parent knows that delayed obedience is really disobedience.

God doesn't owe you an explanation or reason for everything he asks you to do. Understanding can wait, but obedience can't. Instant obedience will teach you more about God than a lifetime of Bible discussions. In fact, you will never understand some commands until you obey them first. Obedience unlocks understanding.

Often we try to offer God partial obedience. We want to pick and choose the commands we obey. We make a list of the commands we like and obey those while ignoring the ones we think are unreasonable, difficult, expensive, or unpopular. I'll attend church but I won't tithe. I'll read my Bible but won't forgive the person who hurt me. Yet partial obedience is disobedience.

Wholehearted obedience is done joyfully, with enthusiasm. The Bible says, "Obey him gladly" (Psalm 100:2a TLB).

This is the attitude of David: "Just tell me what to do and I will do it, Lord. As long as I live I'll wholeheartedly obey" (Psalm 119:33-34 TLB).

James, speaking to Christians, said, "We please God by what we do and not only by what we believe" (James 2:24 CEV).

God's Word is clear that you can't earn your salvation. It comes only by grace, not your effort. But as a child of God you can bring pleasure to your heavenly Father through obedience. Any act of obedience is also an act of worship.

Why is obedience so pleasing to God? Because it proves you really love him. Jesus said, "If you love me, you will obey my commandments" (John 14:15 GNT).

PLAY today's audio teaching from Pastor Rick

Talk It Over

How can you discern when it is God telling you to do something?

In what areas have you displayed partial obedience to God?

How does your attitude toward obedience change when you consider it an act of worship?

CHAPTER TWENTY-SEVEN

JESUS SPOKE IN PARABLES

Why did Jesus speak in parables? What was their purpose?
Parables
The word parable means to "cast alongside" something else, so Jesus used parables in His teachings in this manner. He would cast out a truth alongside an earthly story. Sometimes their purpose was to hide the meaning; sometimes it was to make it plain, but Jesus used parables as an earthly story about a heavenly concept. He was trying to explain the Kingdom of God, so He used physical examples that the people would be familiar with. This was His way of illustrating profound spiritual truths, and they were often tied to the Word of God, but His disciples didn't always understand them, so Jesus needed to explain them, however, in some cases, He choose to hide their meaning.

CHAPTER TWENTY-EIGHT

THE FATHER SPOKE IN PARABLES

SHOW US THE FATHER

John 14:8-10 Philip said to Jesus, "Lord, show us the Father, and it is sufficient for us." Jesus said to him, "Have I been with you so long, and yet you have not known Me, Philip? He who has seen Me has seen the Father; so how can you say, 'Show us the Father'?

The intent of Jesus statement here is clear; Jesus is the same as the Father in nature, existence, and will, and both are God.

Later in John 10:10, Jesus repeated this statement when He told the Pharisees, "I and my Father Are One."

CHAPTER TWENTY-NINE

WHAT WAS A BLOOD COVENANT?

What was a blood covenant (Genesis 15:9-21)?

AThe scene would look quite ominous to modern-day observers—five bloody animal carcasses on the ground, three of them split in half, with the halves separated a short distance from each other. But in Abraham's time it would not have been so menacing. The arrangement of divided animal carcasses would have been instantly recognized as the set-up for making a type of blood covenant.

When God called Abraham out of his hometown and away from all things familiar, He gave Abraham some promises. A covenant is a kind of promise, a contract, a binding agreement between two parties. The fifteenth chapter of Genesis reiterates the covenant God had made with Abraham at his calling. Except this time, God graciously reassures His promise with a visual of His presence. He asks Abraham to find and kill a heifer, a ram, a goat, a dove, and a pigeon. Then, Abraham was to cut them in half (except the birds) and lay the pieces in two rows, leaving a path through the center (Genesis 15:9-10).

In ancient Near Eastern royal land grant treaties, this type of ritual was done to "seal" the promises made. Through this blood covenant, God was confirming primarily three promises He had made to Abraham: the promise of heirs, of land, and of blessings (Genesis 12:2-3). A blood covenant communicated a self-valedictory oath. The parties involved would walk the path between the slaughtered animals so to say, "May this be done to me if I do not keep my oath." Jeremiah 34:18-19 also speaks about this type of oath-making.

However, there was an important difference in the blood oath that God made with Abraham in Genesis 15. When the evening came, God appeared in the form of a "smoking fire pot and flaming torch [that] passed between the pieces" (Genesis 15:17). But Abraham had fallen "into a deep sleep, and a thick and dreadful darkness came over him" (verse 12). Thus, God alone passed through the pieces of dead animals, and the covenant was sealed by God alone. Nothing depended on Abraham. Everything depended on God, who promised to be faithful to His covenant. "When God made his promise to Abraham, since there was no one greater for him to swear by, he swore by himself" (Hebrews 6:13-18). Abraham and his descendants could trust, count on, and believe in everything God promised.

This specific blood covenant is also known as the Abrahamic Covenant. The blood involved in this covenant, as with any blood covenant, signifies the life from which the blood comes (Leviticus 17:11).

The Mosaic Covenant was also a blood covenant in that it required blood to be sprinkled on the tabernacle, "the scroll and all the people" (Hebrews 9:19-21). "In fact, the law requires that nearly everything be cleansed with blood, and without the shedding of blood there is no forgiveness" (Hebrews 9:22). In the Mosaic Covenant, the blood of animals served as a covering, or atonement, for the sins of the people. The animal's life was given in place of the sinner's life. In the Abrahamic Covenant, God, in essence, was declaring He would give His life if His promises were broken. There could be no greater encouragement to believers, since God is eternal and can no more break an oath than He can die.

All of these things were only "copies," or "shadows," of the better covenant to come (Hebrews 9:23). The lives of animals could never remove sin; the life of an animal is not a sufficient substitute for a human life (Hebrews 10:4). The blood of bulls and goats was a temporary appeasement until the final, ultimate blood covenant was made by Jesus Christ Himself – the God Man (Hebrews 9:24-28). The New Covenant was in His blood (Luke 22:20).

The shadows became realities in Christ, who fulfilled all of the Old Testament blood covenants with His own blood. Christians can be confident that the gift of eternal life that God gives through Jesus is the true promise to people of faith. As the apostle Paul explains, the covenant was established with Abraham and his "Seed"—singular. Paul interprets this as the singular person of Christ (Galatians 3:15-16). Therefore, all who are "in Christ" are spiritual heirs of the promises made to Abraham (Galatians 3:29).

To put it simply, a blood covenant is a promise made by God that He will choose a people for Himself and bless them. The covenant was originally for Abraham's physical descendants but was later extended, spiritually, to all those who, like Abraham, believe God (Galatians 3:7; cf. Genesis 15:6). God's promise of eternal blessing is given only on the basis of faith in the saving blood of His Son, Jesus Christ (Hebrews 9:12).

CHAPTER THIRTY

OUR COVENANT IN CHRIST

It is essential for us to understand the importance of covenants in Jesus' faith.

As we hear in today's Genesis reading, the ancient Israelites saw their relationship with Yahweh as a covenant relationship. They were convinced they'd signed a contract with their God. There were specific things they were obligated to do; specific things Yahweh had to do.

We presume Jesus of Nazareth, as a practicing Jew, was also committed to the covenants his faith ancestors had entered into with Yahweh. He never ate pork; his carpenter shop was always closed on the Sabbath.

But we presume he was also committed to the concept of hosed: doing things for God and others that go beyond the covenant's stipulations.

Such actions aren't specifically included in the covenant partners' responsibilities. But if you don't constantly go beyond those responsibilities, history shows that eventually you'll start fudging on them.

It's precisely in his covenant acts of hosed that the Gospel personality of Jesus steps out of the evangelists' narratives. Story after story, saying after saying, parable after parable, we're told Jesus took his covenant with Yahweh beyond just the regulations to which most of his fellow Jews slavishly adhered. His faith in God, demonstrated in his commitment to others, eventually led him to experience God working effectively in the people and situations that filled his everyday life.

It also led him to shutter his shop and hit the road. He morphs into an itinerant preacher, committed to sharing his experience of God's kingdom among us with all he encounters.

His message is short and simple. It takes up just one verse of today's four-verse Gospel: "This is the time of fulfillment. The kingdom of God is at hand. Repent and believe the good news." Jesus was convinced God is among us, working effectively in our daily lives. But unless we repent — change our value system — and make people and their needs the most important part of our existence, we'll never actually experience God working effectively among us.

Just as the rainbow was Yahweh's outward sign of the covenant in Genesis, the author of 1 Peter believes baptism is the outward sign of our joining in Jesus' covenant.

But what about us "cradle Christians" — baptized as infants? Shouldn't we have an eighth sacrament to demonstrate our adult repentance?

We already have such a sacrament: The Eucharist. Every time we celebrate the Lord's Supper we're expected to take part in an outward sign demonstrating our commitment to carry on the ministry and faith of Jesus of Nazareth, a sign in which many Catholics fail to participate — receiving from the cup.

As we'll hear during Holy Thursday's Eucharist, Jesus never thought receiving from the cup was optional — for extra credit.

Notice the words over the cup that Jesus says in that night's 1 Corinthians 11 reading: "This is the cup of the covenant in my blood." Our taking from the cup has something to do with the covenant Jesus made with Yahweh, a covenant that included the hosed that enabled him to reveal God's kingdom around us.

It's possible the historical Jesus endured Good Friday's pain and death only because he was convinced that at least some of his followers would carry on his work. They'd demonstrated their commitment by drinking from his cup.

Can the risen Jesus count on us to make the same commitment?

The Bible tells us that "Jesus has obtained a more excellent ministry, because he is the mediator of a better covenant, which is based on better promises" (Hebrews 8:6-8). This makes us realize that, if we want an involvement with God that accords with God's grace and will, then we must comply with the covenant Jesus Christ has mediated to us.

1 The Covenant's Penalty

If we are not compliant with the covenant mediated by Jesus, then we are "dead in trespasses and sins... sons of disobedience... children of wrath... strangers to the covenants of promise, having no hope and without God in the world" (Ephesians 2:1-3,11-12).

Nobody in their right mind would want to have that kind of relationship with God, would they?

By contrast, if we obey the covenant of Christ, then we "have our access to the Father in one Spirit... no longer aliens and strangers, but fellow citizens with the saints and are of God's household" (Ephesians 2:4-10, Ephesians 2:18-22).

People either accept the covenant and are subject to grace as saints and sons of God through obedience of faith, or they violate the covenant and are subject to wrath as enemies of God through disobedience and unbelief. Either way they are involved with God within the scope of Christ's covenant.

2 The Covenant's Scope

Our right involvement with God is often described as a "covenant relationship with God." The Holy Spirit never speaks of "a covenant relationship". The unscriptural term may be connected to the idea that the covenant of Christ has application only to those who honour it. The Bible's view is quite different...

CHAPTER THIRTY-ONE

THE COVENANT IS MEDIATED TO ALL OF MANKIND

The covenant is mediated to all men.

"There is one mediator between God and men" and he became "a ransom for all" and through him God "desires all men to be saved and to come to a knowledge of the truth" (1Timothy 2:4-6).

How can a covenant not apply to one to whom it has been mediated? To whomever the covenant is mediated, upon them the covenant is binding.

The covenant in Christ's blood applies to all for whom his blood was shed.

Christ's blood is the "blood of the new covenant" (Matthew 26:28). His blood was shed "for the whole world" (1John 2:2).

How can a covenant not apply to one for whom the blood of the covenant was shed? For whomever the blood was shed, to them the covenant is ratified.

The covenant applies to all for whom God confirmed his promise by an oath.

God made a promise to all mankind (John 3:16). God backed up that promise by making an oath to Christ concerning the validity of his high priesthood under the new covenant (Hebrews 6:16-20, cf Hebrews 7:21-22).

How can a covenant not apply to one to whom God has made a promise that the covenant contains and guarantees with an oath? Whoever are able to believe like Abraham the promise and oath of God, to them the covenant applies.

The covenant applies to all who are accountable in the day of judgment.

Christ, at his second coming, will deal out "retribution to those who do not know God and to those who do not obey the gospel of our Lord Jesus" (2Thessalonians 1:8-10).

How can a covenant not apply to one who is condemned for not obeying it? Whoever is accountable for not obeying the covenant, to them the covenant applies.

The covenant dispenses both blessings and curses.

The old covenant, mediated by Moses, contained both "blessings and curses" (Deuteronomy 28:58-63, Deuteronomy 30:9-10,15-20).

The new covenant, mediated by Christ, also contains blessings and curses. Fortunately, the blood of that covenant, Christ's own blood, provides the means of removing its curses and bestowing its blessings (Galatians 3:6-28).

The covenant applies not only to those whom it blesses, but also to those whom it curses so that the curses can be replaced with the blessing.

3 The Covenant's Identity

We need to identify exactly what is the covenant which Christ mediated. I have heard some very complicated answers to that, involving various distinctions, divisions, and dispensations of the word of Christ. However, the correct answer is quite simple. The covenant that Christ mediated is the gospel of Christ.

Paul was unaware of any distinction between the gospel of Christ and the new covenant of Christ. Paul writes to the "beloved of God in Rome, called as saints" and says, "I am eager to preach the gospel to you also who are in Rome" (Romans 1:7,15).

How could this be, if the gospel for sinners and the covenant for saints were two different and separate things? The world is therefore not divided into those who are subject to the gospel and those who are subject to the covenant, for the gospel is the new covenant and all men are subject to it.

Again, Paul refers to "ministers of the new covenant" (2Corinthians 3:6) but later refers to this ministry as the preaching of the gospel (2Corinthians 4:1-6).

Lesson Summary

All men have an involvement with God because the Son of God has shed his blood for all and thereby mediated the new covenant to all.

The gospel of Christ is a covenant which God has made binding on all people, therefore all people are involved with God either as his enemies and under a curse because they reject the gospel, or as his sons and under grace because they accept the gospel.

Our involvement and relationship with God is determined by our covenant with God, a covenant not invented or negotiated by us but mediated to us from God by Christ. We can make sure that we have a right relationship and involvement with God simply by believing and obeying the gospel which God has so graciously provided as the only valid covenant between us and him.

This covenant was ratified by God's own oath and the shed blood of his own Son.

How kind God is to have done this for us, and what fools we are if we do not yield ourselves SPIRIT, SOUL AND BODY to this wonderful covenant with God.

www.ingramcontent.com/pod-product-compliance
Lightning Source LLC
LaVergne TN
LVHW020431080526
838202LV00055B/5138